Panda Panda Bear What Do You Learn: With Jokes and Quizzes

The Blessed Creation

Published by The Blessed Creation, 2023.

While every precaution has been taken in the preparation of this book, the publisher assumes no responsibility for errors or omissions, or for damages resulting from the use of the information contained herein.

PANDA PANDA BEAR WHAT DO YOU LEARN: WITH JOKES AND QUIZZES

First edition. March 7, 2023.

ISBN: 979-8215883556

Written by The Blessed Creation.

Table of Contents

Panda Panda Bear, What Do You Learn: with Jokes and Quizzes

The Blessed Creation

PREFACE

Do you find difficult to teach your children about positive morale, positive attitude, great leadership, to have a great spirit and NOT easy to give up, positive responsibility or something to classify which one is good and which one is bad in our life?

To educate children about anything, especially about morale, attitude and much more are very difficult now days. That's why we need to look seriously into this issue by finding ways and to be more creative way. Through this story in this book, your children will learn about the positive morale, a great leadership, problem solving skills, positive responsibility, great attitude, how to classify which one is good and which one is not good, to have diligent behavior and much more. Through telling this story in this book, you will increase the chances of your children sticking around for whatever else you have to say to educate them seriously but with casual way.

Children's mind are similar like their bodies, as their bodies need healthy food and exercise to advance and grow, their minds need also "the healthy food and exercise", in the form of great ideas and experiences such as by reading this book to advance, to be strong, always having positive attitude, not easy to give up and much more, which are all essential for our life!

We know, it will be more difficult if we teach our children about "Life" if your children have not had any experience with. They may not listen to you (they think you worry too much) or not fully understand you. So experience is great, it will make your children easier to learn and to understand. But reading this book will be the BEST, because your children will learn quickly and having fun on the same time, also stay out from the trouble as well.

Your will like this book because Patrick Panda who had a great memorable adventures is telling your children about what he learned such as:

- How to treat sibling/ friend.
- How to be responsible.
- How and what he learned from His Great Wise Mom about problem solving.
- What he learned from His Wise Mom to become a Good Leader.
- How to be brave and survive.
- What he learned for NOT easy to give up in a difficult situation.
- Patrick stated that he became "The New Patrick" because this memorable experience changed his Life to The BETTER.
- About the diligent behavior and much more.

WE BELIEVE THAT YOU WILL ENJOY THIS BOOK AND OF COURSE YOUR CHILDREN WILL ENJOY AS WELL.

YOU CAN TEACH YOUR CHILDREN WITH THE NEW INNOVATIVE, FUN AND CASUAL WAY AS SOON AS YOU GET THIS BOOK.

CHAPTER I

ABOUT PATRICK FROM the PANDA FAMILY

My name is Patrick, we live in a bamboo forest as a happy family of pandas. My father's name is Peter, my mother's name is Polly, and I have two sisters - Penny, and Piper. I am the only boy, and my sisters Penny and Piper were always teasing me because I was always doing something silly like trying to climb trees, jump from one tree to another tree or swim in the nearby river. I was very naughty boy as well, because I behaved badly and do not do what I was told.

I was told by my parents that I have to tell you about my life story, because recently I got a memorable experience which I need to share. So you will not make the same mistake as I did, also to share what I learned as well.

One day, I wandered off too far and got lost. My mom, my dad and sisters searched for me until they found me after eating fish in a Fish Pond. I didn't know that I wasn't supposed to eat fish belong to our neighbor, and I got in BIG Trouble when my neighbors caught me.

THE BEAUTIFUL FISH POND

*I ATE SEVERAL FISH FROM
THIS FISH POND*

My mom scolded me, but then my mom took care of me when I got
hurt while trying to escape. My Mom cleaned my wounds, gave me some

medication from the doctor and cuddled me until I felt better. After that day, I learned that I needed to be more careful, responsible, and not naughty and listen to my mom's advices.

Eating fish, I thought like eating bamboo shoots. Which is free, apparently not for fish. The owner was angry, hit me with wooden stick. I ran, fell down, I got ankle injury.

I learned a lot of things about "LIFE" from this adventures, I need to share with you.

My mom told me, it will be more difficult if she teach me about "Life" which I have not had any experience with. I may not listen to her or not fully understand her.

So experience is great, it will make me easier to learn. But reading this book will be the BEST, because I reveal what I learned, PLUS you are not getting bruise and ankle injury like me.

Truly after that memorable experience, I become "The New Patrick ", that experience changed my LIFE for the BETTER.

That's why my parents asked me to share about "My memorable experience" with you.

Let me inform you about our family and our daily life first before I reveal about the whole memorable adventures which I had.

Actually we were eating bamboo shoots every day for around 12 hours daily. This is a bit boring, don't you think? I like to eat fish occasionally. My mom told me that I am very naughty boy. I am 17 months now, I like to venture off on my own, but my mum told me to wait another more months.

I would like to inform you about my family:

This is me, Patrick.

These are my sisters, Piper and Penny

By the way, I have some jokes for you:

- What goes black, white, black, and white, black, white?
- Why do pandas like old movies?
- What did the panda say when forced out of its natural habitat?
- What do pandas eat on Halloween?
- What do you call a large group of sick pandas?

> **You will find the answers: on the Chapter VII.**

Sorry, I need to get back to The Story about my family: Every day, we woke up early in the morning to stretch and yawn. We then went out to find our daily food - bamboo shoots! We eat bamboo shoots so much that we could eat up to 50 pounds of it every day! We also loved to munch on fruits like apples and oranges, and sometimes we would snack on little insects we found crawling around.

After breakfast, we liked to take a nice nap in the shade of the bamboo trees. We would cuddle up together and snooze for a few hours, dreaming of all sorts of fun things like climbing trees and playing hide-and-seek.

In the afternoon, we would play together, rolling and tumbling around in the grass. We loved to chase each other and tag, and sometimes we would even dance together in a circle. We were always careful not to hurt each other, and we always made sure everyone was having fun.

We enjoy surfing in the afternoon, especially me, my dad and my mom.

Before the sun began to set, we were playing together. As the sun began to set, we would head back to our cozy bamboo den. My mom, Polly, would tuck us in with a soft blanket and sing a sweet lullaby. Our family would cuddle up together and fall asleep, dreaming of all the adventures we would have the next day.

CHAPTER II

SEVERAL CONFLICTS AMONG THE THREE CHILDREN AND WHAT I LEARNED FROM MY MOM

<u>Who get the last bamboo shoots?</u>

One day, Penny, Piper and myself got into a big fight about who should get the last piece of bamboo shoots for lunch. We were all so hungry and really wanted it, but there was only one piece left! I was being really stubborn and wouldn't let my sisters have it, even though I knew they were just as hungry as myself.

Our mom heard the commotion and came over to see what was going on. She could tell that her cubs were upset and needed some help to resolve the conflict. Our mom sat down with us and asked each of us to explain why we wanted the last piece of bamboo. Penny and Piper explained that they were just as hungry as me and they really wanted to eat too.

I finally realized that I was being selfish and apologized to my sisters for not sharing. My mom praised me for apologizing and reminded all of us how important it is to share and be kind to each other.

In the end, we decided to split the last piece of bamboo into three equal parts so that everyone got a fair share. We all happily ate our lunch together and promised to always share and be kind to each

other in the future.

<u>**Who get the most bamboo shoots?**</u>

Another day, Penny, me and Piper got into a big argument again, about who got to eat the most bamboo shoots. We all wanted the biggest pile for ourselves, and we started pushing and shoving each other. Our mom came to see what was going on and saw the three cubs fighting. Our mom sat us down and said,

"Hey, hey, hey, stop that fighting".

"Fighting never solves anything "

"Now, let's see how we can solve this problem."

She listened to each of us and then came up with a plan that would make everyone happy. She suggested that we all take turns choosing our favorite bamboo shoots from the pile, one at a time. We all agreed, and each of us got to choose our favorite shoot until the pile was gone. We were all happy with the result, and no one got into any more fights.

From that day on, whenever there was a disagreement, our mom taught us to listen to each other and work together to find a solution.

We learned that working together was much better than fighting and that everyone can be happy if we compromise and share.

<u>Who get the toy to play?</u>

Me, Penny, and Piper were playing together when we began to argue over who got to play with a toy. I thought I should have it because I was the biggest, while Penny and Piper thought they should take turns. The argument got louder and louder, and before long, we were shouting at each other.

Our mother, who was nearby, heard the commotion and came over to see what was happening. She listened to each of us and tried to understand our perspectives. She explained that it was important to share and take turns, and that everyone's feelings were important. Then, she came up with a solution that made everyone happy.

She suggested that we take turns playing with the toy, with each of us getting an equal amount of time. She also suggested we come up with a game that we could all play together, so that nobody felt left out. Penny, and Piper also myself thought this was a great idea, and we quickly started playing the new game together. We were having so much fun that we forgot all about our argument.

From that day on, whenever we had a disagreement, we knew we could come to our mother for help. She always listened and helped us find a solution that worked for everyone.

We learned that it was important to talk things out and try to understand each other, and that sometimes, a little compromise can go a long way.

CHAPTER III
ABOUT MY ADVENTUROUS SIDE

I was feeling adventurous and decided to sneak out of my family's bamboo forest home to explore the nearby beach. I wanted to see what was beyond my usual surroundings and what adventures awaited for me.

As I was swimming in the ocean, I noticed a group of seagulls flying around something. Curious, I swam over to see what it was. To my surprise, I found a plastic bag floating in the water. I had heard from my mom that plastic is harmful to the ocean and its creatures. I knew I had to do something to help. I tried to pull the plastic bag out of the water but found it was too heavy for me.

I then remembered my mother's advice about seeking help from others when facing a difficult task. I swam back to shore and asked my family and friends for help. Together, we were able to remove the plastic bag from the water and dispose of it properly. I learned an important lesson that day about the impact of our actions on the environment and the importance of working together to make a difference. I felt proud to have contributed to the well-being of the ocean and its inhabitants. The next day, I decided to explore the beach on my own without telling my family.

I wanders off and gets lost.

At first, I feels excited to be on an adventure, but soon I realizes that I don't know how to get back to my family, because we never have been in this area before. I start to feel scared and worried. Luckily, I remember what my mom taught me about paying attention to my surroundings and using my sense of direction. I looks around and tries to remember which way I came from. I sees some landmarks that I remembers from earlier and uses them to guide me back to my families.

Soon I realizes that I don't know how to get back to my family

When I finally finds my family, they were all relieved to see me. They scolded me for wandering off on my own without telling them first. But also praise me for being brave and finding my way back. I realizes that I should have told my family where I was going, but I also felt proud of myself for using my skills to find my way back.

From this experience, I learned about the importance of staying safe in unfamiliar places and communicating with my family. I also learned that it's okay to be adventurous, but I should always be mindful of my surroundings and make sure to tell someone where I am going. So I have to be responsible and safe.

It is better if I go if somebody else, so if anything happened, we

help each other.

CHAPTER IV

MY ADVENTURE GO WILD by EATING FISH FROM OUR NEIGHBOUR FISH POND

I was a curious and adventurous young panda who loved to explore the world around me. One day, while wandering through my neighborhood, I spotted a beautiful fish pond in my neighbor's backyard. The pond was filled with colorful fish that swam gracefully through the water. I was fascinated and couldn't resist the temptation to take a closer look. I had never seen anything like it before.

As I approached the pond, I noticed that the fish were swimming just beneath the surface. I watched them for a few moments, mesmerized by their movements and the way the sunlight sparkled off their scales. Suddenly, I felt a pang of hunger. I had never tasted fish before, and the idea of trying one was too tempting to resist.

Without thinking, I leaned over the edge of the pond and snatched one of the fish with my jaws. Then I ate the second fish and I ate the third fish. Then I retreated to a nearby tree to enjoy my snack. But I didn't get far before I heard a loud voice shouting my name. Actually I turned to leave, but I was caught in the act by my angry neighbor. The neighbor had been keeping a close eye on the fish pond and was furious to see me snacking on his fish.

It was my neighbor, Mr. Johnson. He was an old and grumpy man who didn't like anyone messing around in his yard. He had seen me take the fish and was furious.

"What do you think you're doing?" he yelled at me.

"That's my fish pond! You have no right to be taking my fish!"

I felt ashamed and embarrassed. I had never intended to cause any harm, but I realized that I had made a BIG mistake. I realized that I had been selfish and short sighted. I had only been thinking about my own hunger and curiosity, without considering the impact that my actions

might have on my neighbor.

I ran as fast as I could, dodging trees and bushes as I tried to escape the angry neighbor. I could hear the neighbor's angry voice and the sound of the stick hitting the ground behind me, making me run even faster. I didn't know where I was going, but I knew I had to get away.

I ran – ran – ran again

As I ran, I stumbled and fell, scraping my paw on a sharp rock. The pain made me cried out, but I quickly got up and continued running.

My first fell down.

I ran and ran and ran again.

I panicked and ran as fast as I could, but I didn't notice the rock on the ground and tripped over it. I fell hard and injured my leg. I tried to get up and run again, but the pain was too much. I crawled behind a bush and hid, hoping Mr. Johnson wouldn't find me.

My second fell down, I twisted my ankle

I could hear the neighbor's footsteps getting closer and closer, and I knew I had to find a place to hide. I saw a nearby tree with a hollow trunk, and I quickly crawled inside. It was dark and cramped, but I was safe for now. I listened as the neighbor ran past, calling out my name in frustration.

After a few minutes, I cautiously emerged from the tree trunk and began making my way back home. I tired and sore from running, but I felt grateful to be alive. When I arrived home, my mother noticed my injuries and asked me what had happened. I told her the whole story, feeling ashamed for my actions. My mother listened patiently and reminded me of the importance of respecting other people's property and being responsible for my actions.

I learned a valuable lesson that day about the consequences of my actions and the importance of making good choices.

CHAPTER V
MY FAMILY LOOKED AFTER ME

While my mom listened to me telling her about the whole story, she cleaned my wounds, put a bandage on my knee, and gave me some medicine to ease the pain. My family also gave me plenty of food and water to help me recover as soon as possible.

I felt grateful to my family for taking care of me and to Mr. Johnson for not hitting me.

As my mom tended to me, she talked to me about what had happened. She told me that my actions had consequences, and that I needed to take responsibility for what I had done. She explained that taking something that didn't belong to me was wrong, and that it hurt other people. Meanwhile, my mom had been caring for me and helping me to recover from my injury. She had used the time to talk to me about my actions and to teach me about the importance of making things right when I had done something wrong.

My dad was also concerned about my injury as well. He asked me what had happened, and I explained that I had taken a fish from Mr. Johnson's pond and was caught, which led to me falling and injuring my leg.

My dad was disappointed in my behavior, but he also understood that I was young and curious, and that I needed to be taught the right way to explore the world around me. He explained to me that it was important to respect other people's property and not take things without permission.

My family took turns taking care of me and keeping me company while I rested. They brought me my favorite foods and read me stories to help me feel better. I was grateful for their care and love. My ankle injury turned out to be more serious than we thought. I had a bad sprain and needed to stay off my feet for a few days. While I was stuck at home, my mom took care of me and tried to keep my spirits up. She knew that I was feeling guilty and ashamed about what I had done to Mr. Johnson's fish pond.

There was a day which I always remember, when I was feeling particularly down, my mom came into my room with a surprise. She had brought me a small fish tank with a couple of goldfish in it.

"Patrick, I know you feel bad about what happened with Mr. Johnson's fish pond," she said.

"But I want to show you that there is a right way to enjoy and care for fish. These little guys need your love and attention just like the fish in Mr. Johnson's pond."

I was surprised and touched by my mom's gesture. I started taking care of the fish, feeding them and cleaning their tank. As I watched them swim around, I realized how much joy and peace they brought me.

My Mom gave me some advices.

My Dad also gave me some advices.

I felt ashamed and sorry for what I had done, but I also felt comforted by my mother's care and understanding. I knew that she loved me and wanted me to learn from my mistake. Over the next few days, I stayed home from school to recover from my injury. My mother made sure that I had everything I needed and checked on me often to make sure I was okay.

I also felt my mother's care and understanding.

During this time, I thought a lot about what my mom had said to me. I realized that I needed to make things right with Mr. Johnson and to apologize for my actions. As my leg slowly healed, I spent my time reflecting on my actions and planning how I could make things right with Mr. Johnson. Hopefully I gathered my courage and apologized to Mr. Johnson in person, promising never to take his fish again.

When I was feeling better, I decided to go and talk to Mr. Johnson again. I went to Mr. Johnson's house and knocked on his door. Mr. Johnson answered, looking surprised to see me. I nervously apologized to Mr. Johnson for taking his fish and causing trouble. I explained that I had been curious and didn't think about the consequences of my actions. I promised never to take anything without permission again.

Despite my sincere apology, Mr. Johnson did not accept it. He was still angry at me for taking his fish and causing trouble. He felt that my behavior was unacceptable and that I needed to be punished. I was disappointed that my apology was not accepted, but I also understood why Mr. Johnson was upset. I knew that I had made a mistake and that I needed to make things right.

I decided to try again to apologize to Mr. Johnson. I wrote him a letter expressing my regret for my actions and explaining how sorry I was. I also offered to help Mr. Johnson in any way I could to make things right. Mr. Johnson received the letter and was touched by my words. He began to see that I was truly sorry and that I had learned my lesson. He decided to give me a second chance and invited me over to talk. When I arrived, Mr. Johnson sat down with me and talked about what had happened. He explained why he was upset and how my behavior had caused problems. I listened carefully and apologized again for my actions.

Finally, Mr. Johnson accepted my apology and forgave me. He also thanked me for my offer to help and accepted my help in taking care of the fish pond. After this day, I and Mr. Johnson worked together to maintain the fish pond and developed a friendship based on mutual respect and understanding.

I had learned that it's important to take responsibility for one's actions and to make amends when things go wrong. I also learned that forgiveness and second chances are possible, even when mistakes are made. I was more careful about my actions and more thoughtful about how my behavior affected others. I knew that my mother and my family was always there for me, to love me and guide me, no matter what.

We are The Happy Family Again.

CHAPTER VI

PATRICK LEARNED A LOT OF LESSONS FROM THIS ADVENTURE

There are a lot of lessons which I learned from this adventure:

- **Respect for others**: My curiosity led me to take fish from my neighbor's pond without permission. This is disrespectful behavior, and I learned the importance of respecting other people's property and boundaries.
- **Honesty**: When I was caught, I initially lied to Mr. Johnson. However, I learned that lying only makes things worse and that honesty is always the best policy.
- **Consequences**: I learned that every action has consequences, both good and bad. I realized that I must be prepared to face the consequences of my actions, whether they are positive or negative.
- **Patience**: When Mr. Johnson was angry with me, I had to be patient and wait for him to calm down before I could apologize. I learned that sometimes it takes time for people to forgive, and that patience is key in repairing damaged relationships.
- **Empathy**: Throughout my adventure, I learned to see things from other people's perspectives. I realized that my actions affected others and that it was important to consider their feelings and needs.

- **Not easy to give up**: I tried to make amends with my neighbor by apologizing, but my neighbor was still angry and did not accept my apology. I realizes that sometimes, no matter how much you apologize, some people may not be ready to forgive you right away. Feeling frustrated and upset, I turned to my family for comfort. They encouraged me to keep trying to make things right and not to give up. They also remind me that it's important to learn from my mistakes and to try to be a better person in the future. I sent an apology letter to him and offering to help with his Fish Pond.

Finally, my neighbor started to see that I was genuinely sorry and was trying to make things right. Slowly but surely, the neighbor began to forgive me and we started to build a better relationship. Through this experience, I learned that making mistakes is part of our life, but it's important to take responsibility for our actions and try to make things right. I also learned that sometimes forgiveness takes time, and that's okay. It's important to keep trying and to never give up on making things right.

- **Overall,** my adventure was a lesson-filled experiences, taught me many valuable life lessons that can help me become a better person. By learning from my mistakes, I was able to grow and develop important skills that will serve me well throughout my life.

Through my adventures and misadventures, I learned about the importance of honesty, communication, and respecting other people's property. In the end, I had grown as a person and had become more thoughtful and responsible.

I knew that I could always count on my mother's love and guidance to help me through life's challenges. So I am very happy now, my family is reunited and I have learned valuable lessons that will help me grow into a responsible and respectful panda. My family can enjoy a meal together and reflect on my experiences.

CHAPTER VII
ABOUT PANDA'S JOKES

> **These are the answers of the jokes from the previous chapter:**

1. A panda rolling down a hill.
2. Because they're in black and white.
3. This is un - bear- able
4. Bam-boo
5. A panda-emic

> **We have more Panda jokes and the answers for you:**

1.   Why did the panda join a circus?

Answer: Because he wanted to learn how to juggle bamboo sticks!

1.   What do you get when you cross a panda and a koala?

Answer: A "pandala"!

1.   What do you call a panda who just woke up?

Answer: A "pandawake"!

1. What do pandas eat for breakfast?

Answer: "Pandakes"!

1. Why did the panda go to the doctor?

Answer: Because he had a bamboo-tummy!

1. What do you call a panda who can speak two languages?

Answer: A "pandalingual"!

1. Why did the panda become a vegetarian?

Answer: Because he didn't want to "herbivore" problems!

1. What do you call a panda who loves to swim?

Answer: A "pandaswim"!
9. Why do pandas love bamboo so much?
Answer: Because it's "pandarific"!
10. What do you call a group of pandas playing hide and seek?
Answer: A "pandamaze"!
11. How do pandas keep their teeth clean?
Answer: They use "panda-toothpaste"!
12. Why did the panda refuse to go to the zoo?
Answer: Because he didn't want to be "panda-monium"!
13. What do you call a panda who loves to travel?
Answer: A "pandaventurer"!
14. What do you call a panda who is always on time?
Answer: A "pandaclock"!
15. Why did the panda cross the road twice?
Answer: Because he was a "panda-dext"!

16. What do you call a panda who loves to sing?
Answer: A "pandasong"!
17. Why did the panda wear a hat?
Answer: To keep his head "panda-warm"!
18. What do you call a panda who loves to dance?
Answer: A "pandancer"!
19. Why did the panda go to space?
Answer: To eat "panda-stronaut" ice cream!
20. What do you call a panda who loves to read?
Answer: A "pandaliterate"!
21. Why did the panda join a gym?
Answer: To become a "panda-muscle"!
22. What do you call a panda who loves to play soccer?
Answer: A "pandasoccer"!
23. Why did the panda refuse to climb a mountain?
Answer: Because he was afraid of "panda-falling"!
24. What do you call a panda who loves to draw?
Answer: A "pandartist"!
25. Why did the panda visit the doctor?
Answer: Because he was feeling "pandasick"!
26. What do you call a panda who loves to play the piano?
Answer: A "pianopanda"!
27. Why did the panda love to take pictures?
Answer: Because he wanted to create "panda-memories"!
28. What do you call a panda who loves to watch movies?
Answer: A "pandafilm"!
29. Why do pandas love old movies?
Answer: Because they are in black and white, just like pandas!
30. Why did the panda refuse dessert?
Answer: Because he was already stuffed!
31. What did the panda say when he was offered a sandwich?
Answer: "No thanks, I only eat bamboo shoots."

32. Why did the panda wear a tuxedo?
Answer: Because he was going to a black and white ball.

33. Why did the panda go to school?

Answer: To become a "pandascholar"!
34. What do you call a panda who loves to play video games?
Answer: A "pandagamer"!
35. Why did the panda love to go on hikes?
Answer: To enjoy the "panda-rama"!

36. What do you call a panda who loves to play chess?

Answer: A "pandachess"!

37. Why did the panda become a detective?

Answer: To solve "panda-mysteries"!

38. What do you call a panda who loves to bake?

Answer: A "pandabaker"!
39. Why did the panda love to play basketball?
Answer: Because he could "panda-dunk"!
40. What do you call a panda who loves to paint?
Answer: A "pandapainter"!
41. Why did the panda become a scientist?
Answer: To study "panda-nature"!
42. What do you call a panda who loves to ride roller coasters?
Answer: A "pandacoaster"!
43. Why did the panda join a choir?
Answer: To sing "panda-harmony"!
44. What do you call a panda who loves to do magic tricks?
Answer: A "pandamagician"!

45. Why did the panda go to the beach?
Answer: To enjoy the "panda-sand"!
46. What do you call a panda who loves to write stories?
Answer: A "pandawriter"!
47. Why did the panda become a firefighter?
Answer: To put out "panda-flames"!
48. What do you call a panda who loves to ride roller skates?
Answer: A "pandaskater"!
49. Why did the panda love to play musical instruments?
Answer: Because he was "panda-talented"!
50. What do you call a panda who loves to take naps?
Answer: A "pandanapper"!
51. Why did the panda love to watch movies?
Answer: To enjoy "panda-rama"!
52. What do you call a panda who loves to dance?
Answer: A "pandancer"!
53. Why did the panda become a musician?
Answer: To play "panda-monium"!
54. What do you call a panda who loves to play soccer?
Answer: A "pandasoccer"!
55. Why did the panda go to space?
Answer: To explore "panda-planets"!
56. What do you call a panda who loves to draw?
Answer: A "pandartist"!
57. Why did the panda love to eat bamboo?
Answer: Because it was "panda-licious"!
58. What do you call a panda who loves to read books?
Answer: A "pandareader"!
59. Why did the panda become a chef?
Answer: To cook up some "panda-cakes"!
60. What do you call a panda who loves to do puzzles?
Answer: A "pandapuzzler"!

61. Why did the panda become a comedian?

Answer: To tell some "panda-jokes"!

62. What do you call a panda who loves to swim?

Answer: A "pandaswimmer"!

63. Why did the panda become a veterinarian?

Answer: To take care of "panda-imals"!

64. What do you call a panda who loves to play the guitar?

Answer: A "pandaguitarist"!

65. Why did the panda love to go to the amusement park?

Answer: To ride some "panda-ful" rides!

66. What do you call a panda who loves to do gymnastics?

Answer: A "pandagymnast"!

67. Why did the panda become a pilot?

Answer: To fly over "panda-mountains"!

68. What do you call a panda who loves to write poetry?

Answer: A "pandapoet"!

69. Why did the panda love to go to the circus?

Answer: To see some "panda-tastic" acts!

70. What do you call a panda who loves to play with toys?

Answer: A "pandaplayful"!

71. Why did the panda become a teacher?

Answer: To educate some "panda-cubs"!

72. What do you call a panda who loves to do yoga?

Answer: A "pandayogi"!

73. Why did the panda become an astronaut?

Answer: To float in "panda-space"!

74. What do you call a panda who loves to tell stories?

Answer: A "pandastoryteller"!

75. Why did the panda love to go to the park?

Answer: To play on the "panda-grounds"!

76. How do you know if a panda has a cold?

Answer: He'll be "a-sneezy"!

77. What do you call a group of pandas singing together?

Answer: A pandamonium!

78. Why did the panda cross the road?

Answer: To get to the bamboo on the other side!

79. What do pandas use to keep their beds clean?

Answer: Panda-paws!

80. What do you get when you cross a panda and a polar bear?

Answer: A "bipolar" bear!

81. How do pandas ride bikes?

Answer: They use their "panda-dles"!

82. What do you call a panda who loves music?

Answer: A rock-a-panda!

83. What do you call a panda that does kung fu?

Answer: A kung-fu-panda!

84. Why did the panda climb up the tree?

Answer: To get away from the bamboo-zled tiger!

85. How do pandas make pancakes?

Answer: They use bamboocakes!

CHAPTER VIII

ABOUT THE FIRST PATRICK'S SISTER, PIPER

In a lush bamboo forest nestled in the mountains of China, a baby panda was born. The little panda was small and helpless, with soft, fluffy black and white fur, and big, round eyes that sparkled with curiosity. Its mother, named Polly, she was a gentle giant panda, carefully cradled the newborn in her arms, licked it with her soft pink tongue and nuzzled it affectionately. The baby panda's eyes were closed, but it could hear the sound of its mother's heartbeat and feel the warmth of her body, and it knew that it was safe and loved.

As the days passed, the baby panda, named Piper grew stronger and more adventurous. It loved to explore its surroundings, climbing trees and playing with its siblings, Patrick and Penny. It also enjoyed snacking on bamboo shoots and leaves, which made up the majority of its diet.

As Piper grew older, it became more independent and began to explore further away from its mother's side. It learned how to forage for food on its own, and spent more time playing with other pandas in the forest. The panda communicated with its peers through a series of grunts, bleats, and other vocalizations, as well as through body language such as playful nudges and head tilts.

As Piper entered adulthood, it began to seek out a mate and establish its own territory within the forest. It continued to eat bamboo, but also added other foods to its diet such as fruits, nuts, and small animals like rodents and birds. It built a cozy den in a hollow tree trunk, where it could rest and sleep during the day.

Over the years, Piper grew old and began to slow down. Its once sleek fur had become gray and patchy, and its movements were more sluggish. But despite its advanced age, the panda remained a beloved member of the forest community, and continued to play an important role in maintaining the delicate balance of the ecosystem.

As the panda reached the end of its long life, it reflected on all the joys and challenges it had experienced over the years. It thought about the many friends it had made, the delicious foods it had tasted, and the beautiful sights it had seen in the forest. It also thought about the struggles it had faced, such as competition for food and mates, and the ever-present danger of predators.

Despite the challenges, the panda knew that its life had been full of love, laughter, and adventure. It closed its eyes and peacefully drifted off to sleep, surrounded by the gentle rustling of the bamboo leaves and the soothing sounds of the forest. And though Piper was gone, its legacy lived on in the hearts and memories of all those who had known and loved it.

And when the time came for the panda to leave this world, it did so with dignity and grace. It lay down in a peaceful clearing, surrounded by its family and friends, and closed its eyes for the final time. And though its physical form was gone, its spirit lived on in the hearts and memories of all those who had known and loved it. The panda had lived a full and joyful life, and it had left its mark on the world in countless ways.

CHAPTER IX

ABOUT THE SECOND PATRICK'S SISTER, PENNY

In the bamboo forests of Sichuan, China, the second Patrick's sister, Penny was born.

Penny was unlike any other panda in her community. She was small and fragile, and had a curious nature that often got her into trouble.

When Penny was still a cub, she wandered too far from her mother's side and got lost. She spent two days alone in the forest, scared and hungry, before she was finally rescued by a group of kind hearted monkeys. From that moment on, Penny knew that the world was full of dangers and she had to be careful.

As Penny grew up, she faced many challenges. She had a hard time finding enough food to eat, as the bamboo forests were slowly disappearing due to human development. Penny also had to learn how to defend herself from predators, such as leopards and wild dogs that roamed the forests.

But Penny was determined to survive. She learned how to climb trees and navigate the forest with ease. She also became an expert at finding alternative sources of food, such as berries, nuts, and insects. Penny even befriended a group of playful otters, who would sometimes help her find food and play with her in the river.

Despite her many challenges, Penny never lost her sense of wonder and curiosity. She would often venture far beyond the bamboo forests, exploring new landscapes and meeting new creatures. On one such adventure, Penny stumbled upon a group of endangered red pandas, who were in desperate need of help. Penny spent several weeks caring for the sick and injured animals, nursing them back to health and teaching them how to survive in the wild.

Penny's bravery and kindness did not go unnoticed. She became known as a respected leader in the forest, and other animals would often come to her for help and advice. Penny also took on the role of teacher, passing on her knowledge and skills to younger generations of pandas. Penny had a lot of talent like her mom, Polly.

As Penny grew older, she began to feel the effects of aging. Her joints became stiff, and she could no longer climb trees or run as fast as she used to. Penny was saddened by her physical limitations, but she refused to let them slow her down. She continued to explore the world around her, using her wisdom and experience to guide her on new adventures.

When Penny finally passed away, she left behind a legacy of courage, kindness, and adventure. Her spirit lived on in the forests she had loved so much, and her story inspired generations of pandas to come. Penny had faced many challenges throughout her life, but she had never given up.

She had always persevered, and had made the most of every moment she had been given.

CHAPTER X
ABOUT PANDA QUIZZES

1. What is the scientific name for pandas?
2. Where do giant pandas live?
3. What do pandas eat?
4. How much bamboo can a panda eat in one day?
5. What color are a panda's eyes?
6. How big can pandas grow to be?
7. How long can pandas live in the wild?
8. Are pandas social animals?
9. Do pandas hibernate?

10. What is the average weight of an adult panda?

11. What is a group of pandas called?

12. What is the name of the famous panda who lived in the San Diego Zoo?

13. What is the name of the famous panda who lived in the Washington National Zoo?

14. What is the name of the famous panda who lived in the Berlin Zoo?

15. What is the name of the famous panda who lived in the Chengdu Panda Base?

16. How long is a panda's tail?

17. What is the name of the black and white pattern on a panda's fur?

18. How fast can pandas run?

19. Are panda's good swimmers?

20. How many toes do pandas have?

21. What is the name of the substance that pandas use to mark their territory?

22. How long do pandas spend each day eating?

23. Do pandas have any natural predators?

24. How many cubs can a female panda have at one time?

25. What is the gestation period of a panda?

26. How long does it take for a panda cub to open its eyes?

27. How long does it take for a panda cub to start eating bamboo?

28. At what age do panda cubs become independent?

29. What is the name of the process by which pandas digest bamboo?

30. How do pandas communicate with each other?

31. How many pandas are estimated to be left in the wild?

32. How many pandas are estimated to be in captivity?

33. What is the name of the organization dedicated to protecting pandas and their habitat?

34. How much land is protected for pandas in China?

35. What is the name of the mountain range where pandas live in the wild?

Here are the answers to the 35 panda quiz questions:

1. Ailuropoda melanoleuca
2. China, specifically Sichuan, Shaanxi, and Gansu provinces
3. Bamboo
4. Up to 40 kg (88 lbs)
5. Black
6. Up to 1.8 m (6 ft) long and 150 kg (330 lbs) in weight
7. Up to 20 years
8. No, they are generally solitary animals
9. No, but they do reduce their activity levels during the winter

10. Around 70 - 125 kg (154 - 275 lbs)

11. A "sleuth" or "embarrassment"

12. Bai Yun

13. Mei Xiang

14. Bao Bao

15. Tai Shan

16. Around 10 - 15 cm (4 - 6 in)

17. "Panda pattern" or "panda bear markings"

18. Up to 32 km/h (20 mph)

19. Yes, they are good swimmers

20. There are 6 toes on their front paws and 5 on their back paws

21. Scent marking with a substance called "pheromones"

22. Up to 16 hours

23. Snow leopards and yellow-throated martens

24. Around 1 - 3 cubs

25. Around 95 - 160 days

26. Around 6 - 8 weeks

27. Around 6 - 12 months

28. Around 18 months

29. Fermentation

30. Vocalizations such as bleats, honks, and growls

31. About 1,800 in the wild

32. About 600 in captivity

33. The World Wildlife Fund (WWF)

34. Over 20,000 km2 (7,722 sq mi)

35. The Qinling Mountains

CHAPTER XII
MOM AND DAD STORY

I am Patrick's Mom, I would like to tell you about our memorable life stories about our family.

<u>Our Children Looked After Themselves</u>

As you remember we had three adorable cubs - two girls, Piper and Penny, and our eldest one, Patrick. We were loving parents who adored our children, but we were also realistic. We knew that as the cubs grew up, they would have to learn to look after themselves and each other. Me, Mama Panda had grown up with five siblings myself, and knew the importance of siblings helping each other out.

So we made a plan to teach our cubs how to care for each other. We started with small tasks, like having Piper help Penny with her bamboo shoots, and having Patrick help me carry water from the stream. We praised their cubs when they helped each other out, and gently corrected them when they didn't.

At first, the cubs were hesitant to help each other. They were used to being taken care of by us, and didn't quite understand why they had to help each other out. But we persevered, and eventually the cubs started to get the hang of it.

We had to go out of the forest to gather more bamboo. We knew it was time for their cubs to take on more responsibility, so we left them with a list of tasks to complete. Piper was in charge of making sure Penny didn't wander too far from the den, Patrick was responsible for collecting firewood, and Penny had to keep watch for any predators.

The cubs were nervous at first, but they knew they had to step up and take care of each other. Piper and Penny worked together to gather bamboo shoots, while Patrick scoured the forest for dry twigs and branches. Penny kept a watchful eye on the surroundings, making sure no predators were lurking nearby.

Then the cubs grew tired and hungry. But they didn't give up. Piper suggested they take a break and share the bamboo shoots they had collected. Patrick built a small fire and they roasted the shoots, savoring the warmth and the taste.

We returned to the den that evening to find our cubs happy and healthy, and proud of what we had accomplished. We knew our plan to teach our cubs how to take care of each other was working.

Over time, the cubs grew more and more confident in their abilities to care for each other. Piper and Penny would often help each other with their fur, making sure they were always clean and well-groomed. Patrick would often carry Penny on his back when she got tired on long walks. Of course, there were still moments of sibling squabbles and disagreements. But we taught our cubs to talk things out and compromise. We also made sure to praise their cubs when they did something kind or helpful for each other. As the cubs grew older, they continued to take care of each other. Piper became the caretaker of the family, making sure everyone had enough to eat and was well-rested. Penny became the protector, always on the lookout for danger. And Patrick became the adventurer, always eager to explore new parts of the forest.

We were proud of our cubs, and knew we had done a good job in teaching them how to care for each other. We watched as our cubs grew into strong, independent pandas, who were always there for each other, no matter what.

<u>Fierce Storm Swept Through the Bamboo Forest</u>

A fierce storm swept through the bamboo forest. The wind howled, the rain poured down, and lightning lit up the sky. We knew we had to take shelter, but we were worried about our cubs.

All of our children had all gone out to play, and we had lost sight of them in the chaos of the storm. We searched everywhere for our cubs, calling out their names and hoping for a response.

Finally, we heard a faint cry coming from a nearby cave. It was Patrick, who had been exploring and had gotten trapped by a rock slide. We rushed to the cave and tried to move the rocks, but the rocks were too heavy. We knew we had to get help, but we couldn't leave Patrick alone in the dark cave. So we sent Penny and Piper to go and find other pandas who could help us. Penny and Piper were nervous, but they knew they had to be brave for their brother. They set out into the storm, calling out for help. They searched high and low, through the rain and the wind, until they finally found a group of pandas who were willing to help. The pandas rushed to the cave and started moving the rocks. It was a slow and difficult process, but we worked together and eventually managed to free Patrick. We were overjoyed to see their cubs safe and sound, and we thanked the other pandas for their help.

From this experience our children knew just how important it was to take care of each other. We had saved each other's lives, and that was a bond that could never be broken.

Our Each Children Personalities and Interests

As our children grew up, they started to develop their own personalities and interests. Piper was outgoing and loved to explore new places, Penny was creative and enjoyed making art, and Patrick was quiet and thoughtful, often lost in his own world. We were proud of our cubs and encouraged them to follow their passions. We knew that each of our children had their own unique strengths and talents, and we wanted to help them grow and thrive.

One particular day, Piper came home with an exciting announcement. She had been invited to go on an adventure with some other young pandas from the forest, and she couldn't wait to go. We were a little worried about our daughter going off on her own, but we knew we had to let her follow her dreams. Before she left, we gave her some advice.

"Remember, Piper," we said, "you have two siblings who love you and will always be there for you. If you ever need anything, don't hesitate to reach out to them."

Piper nodded, hugged her parents and said goodbye, and set off into the forest with her new friends. They explored new territories, climbed trees, and even met some other animals, like a friendly fox and a wise old owl. But as the days went by, Piper started to feel homesick. She missed her family and her familiar surroundings. She tried to push the feelings away, but they kept nagging at her. Finally, she couldn't take it anymore. She gathered her courage and called her siblings on her mobile, she had brought along.

"Penny, Patrick, it's me, Piper," she said. "I miss you guys so much. I wish you were here with me."

Penny and Patrick were overjoyed to hear from their sister. They had been worried about her, but they didn't want to intrude on her adventure.

"Piper, we're here for you," Penny said. "Whatever you need, we'll do our best to help."

Piper felt a weight lifted off her shoulders. She knew that no matter how far away she was, her family would always be there for her. She continued her adventure, but now with a newfound sense of comfort and security. When she returned home, we were waiting for her with open arms. We were thrilled to hear about her adventures, but also proud of her for reaching out to her siblings when she needed them. From then on, Piper, Penny, and Patrick made sure to stay in touch regularly, whether through telephone or visits. They knew that no matter what life threw their way, they had each other to rely on.

<u>A Vacation Together to the Beach</u>

Our family decided to take a vacation together to the beach. It was a long drive, but we packed plenty of snacks and games to keep us occupied on the way. When we arrived, we were awestruck by the vast expanse of sand and sea stretching out before us. The cubs couldn't wait to explore, while myself and Papa Panda set up a cozy spot on the beach with umbrellas and towels.

For the first few days, everything was perfect. The family played in the water, built sandcastles, and ate delicious seafood at the local restaurants. But on the fourth day, things took a turn.

Patrick was out swimming in the ocean when he got caught in a strong current. He tried to swim back to shore, but it was too strong. He started to panic and shout for help. We heard our son's cries and quickly realized what was happening. We knew we had to act fast. My husband grabbed a life ring and ran into the water, while I alerted the lifeguards. Together, we managed to bring Patrick back to shore safely. He was shaken up but unharmed, thanks to the quick thinking and bravery which we did. The incident shook our family up, but it also brought us even closer together. We realized how important it was to look out for each other and to always be prepared for the unexpected.

For the rest of the vacation, we took extra precautions to make sure everyone stayed safe. We swam closer to shore, wore life vests, and made sure to check in with each other regularly. As the vacation came to a close, our family looked back on our time at the beach with mixed emotions. We had experienced both joy and fear, but ultimately, we had grown stronger as a family.

We returned home with a newfound appreciation for each other and a deeper understanding of the importance of safety and preparedness. The next time we went on vacation, we knew we would be ready for anything that came our way. Our panda family continued to face challenges and adventures over the years, but we always faced them together, with love and support for each other. We were a true testament to the power of family and the strength that can come from looking out for each other.

<u>Our Home Was Covered in a Thick Layer of Snow</u>

One winter day, our panda family woke up to find that our home was covered in a thick layer of snow. The cubs, Patrick, Piper and Penny were thrilled and immediately begged their parents to take them outside to play. I and my husband agreed, but only on the condition that they bundle up properly and stick together. They knew that playing in the snow could be dangerous, especially for young cubs. All of our children were overjoyed as they played in the snow, building snowmen and having snowball fights. But as the day wore on, the snow started to get deeper and the temperature dropped even further.

Suddenly, Penny fell into a deep snowdrift and couldn't get out. She started to panic, and her cries for help were muffled by the snow. My husband sprang into action, using his strong arms to dig Penny out of the snowdrift. I comforted Penny, making sure she was okay.

After the incident, we sat down with our cubs and had a serious conversation about the importance of safety in the winter. We explained how to avoid getting lost in the snow, what to do if someone fell into a snowdrift, and how to stay warm.

From that day on, the panda family always made sure to prepare properly before playing outside in the winter. We wore warm clothing, stayed in sight of each other, and never strayed too far from home. The incident with Penny also brought the family even closer together. The children realized that even in the midst of fun and games, safety should always be the top priority. As they snuggled up together by the fire that night, we knew that we had once again taught our cubs an important lesson about the power of family and the importance of looking out for each other.

We Stumbled Upon a Group of Animals That We Had Never Seen Before

Piper and Penny were playing in the forest near their home when they stumbled upon a group of animals that they had never seen before. They were small and furry, with long bushy tails and bright eyes. Piper and Penny were curious, but they didn't know if the animals were friendly or not. They decided to go back and ask us for advice. We listened carefully as Piper and Penny described the animals they had seen. We recognized them as red pandas, a species that lived in the forest nearby.

We explained that red pandas were harmless and friendly, but it was important to always be cautious around new animals. We also suggested that Piper and Penny introduce themselves and try to make friends with the red pandas. Piper and Penny were nervous at first, but they mustered up the courage to approach the red pandas. They introduced themselves and struck up a conversation, and soon they were laughing and playing together.

As the day wore on, we grew worried about Piper and Penny. We went out into the forest to search for our cubs, and when we found them playing with the red pandas, they were relieved. The panda family spent the rest of the day playing with the red pandas, learning more about their habits and way of life. They discovered that despite their differences, they had much in common, and they formed a deep bond. As they walked home that evening, Piper and Penny were overjoyed. They had made new friends and learned an important lesson about acceptance and tolerance.

We were proud of our cubs and the way we had handled the situation. We knew that we had taught them an important lesson about the power of friendship and the importance of respecting others.

I Had a Cough and a Runny Nose and Felt Weak and Tired

I woke up feeling under the weather. I had a cough and a runny nose and felt weak and tired. My husband knew that he had to step up and take care of the family. He spent the day cooking meals, cleaning the house, and looking after our children. He even made sure to keep my favorite soup hot and ready for when I felt better.

Our children were impressed by their father's efforts. They had never seen him work so hard before. They asked him if he needed any help, but he insisted that they focus on their schoolwork and playtime. As the days passed, my condition worsened. I had a high fever and was too weak to get out of bed. My husband knew that he needed to get my medical attention, but he didn't want to leave the cubs alone. He decided to take them with him to the hospital. They waited patiently in the waiting room as I was examined by the doctor.

After a few hours, the doctor emerged from the exam room with a prescription for medicine and some advice for him on how to care for me. My husband followed the doctor's instructions carefully, making sure that I took my medicine on time and stayed comfortable. He also made sure that the cubs continued with their routine, attending school and playing with their friends.

Days turned into weeks, and I slowly began to recover. I was grateful for the love and care that my husband had shown her and their cubs during her illness. Our family emerged from this experience even stronger than before. We had learned that even in the toughest of times, they could rely on each other for support and care. As we sat down for a family meal one evening, I looked around at her husband and cubs with pride. I knew that they were a strong and loving family, and that no matter what life through our way, we would always face it together.

A Picnic in the Forest

One sunny afternoon, we decided to take our children and their friends on a picnic in the forest. We packed a basket full of delicious snacks and drinks and set off on the short hike to our favorite spot. As we settled down on a blanket, we noticed that our children were being extra helpful and friendly to their friends. They made sure everyone had a seat, offered to share their snacks, and even helped set up a game of Frisbee.

We were proud of our cubs and the way they were being kind and inclusive to their friends. We knew that it wasn't always easy to share and be considerate, but it was an important lesson to learn. As the day wore on, Patrick and his friend began to notice the beauty and richness of the forest around them. They pointed out the different trees, flowers, and animals that they had never noticed before. We smiled as we watched the children explore and discover the wonders of nature. We knew that these moments were precious and important, and we were happy to be able to share them with their family and friends.

As the sun began to set, the panda family and their friends packed up their things and started the short hike back home. Our children's friends thanked us for a wonderful day and said that they couldn't wait to do it again. We knew that the day had been a success. We had taught our cubs an important lesson about kindness and sharing, and they had given their friends a chance to appreciate the beauty and diversity of nature. As we walked home, Piper and Penny chatted excitedly about their next adventure. We smiled, knowing that their cubs were growing up to be kind, curious, and adventurous young pandas.

Wanted to Cool Off in the Nearby River

It was a hot summer day, our children wanted to cool off in the nearby river. We were hesitant at first, worried about the safety of our cubs in the water, but we agreed to take them as long as they promised to be careful. The children squealed with excitement as they splashed and played in the refreshing water. We watched from a distance, keeping a watchful eye on our cubs. Suddenly, Piper slipped on a slippery rock and fell into the deep part of the river. She quickly shouted for help, and Patrick and Penny swam over to assist.

We rushed over to see what had happened. We were relieved to see that Piper was okay but shaken from the experience. We used this as an opportunity to teach the children about water safety. We explained the importance of wearing life jackets and being aware of the depth and speed of the water. Our children listened intently, realizing that they had not been as careful as they should have been. They thanked us for the lesson and promised to be more cautious in the future.

The children continued to play in the water, but this time with a new sense of awareness and responsibility. We watched with pride as our cubs put their new knowledge into practice. When it was time to go home, we gathered the children together and praised them for their responsible behavior. We reminded them that safety always came first and that they should never be afraid to ask for help if they needed it. Our children knew that they had learned an important lesson about water safety, and they were grateful to have such caring and responsible parent to guide them.

Patrick Suddenly Sneezed and Complained of Feeling Feverish

It was a lazy Sunday morning, and Patrick, Piper, and their younger sibling, Penny were lounging around in their pajamas. We had gone out to run some errands, leaving the cubs in charge of the house. As they watched cartoons on the TV, Patrick suddenly sneezed and complained of feeling feverish. Piper and Penny jumped into action, fetching him a glass of water and some tissues. Patrick looked up at his siblings with a grateful smile, feeling comforted by their care and attention.

Piper and Penny knew that they had to take care of their brother while their parents were away, and they were determined to do it well. They rummaged through the kitchen pantry, looking for something to cook for lunch. Piper suggested making dumplings, but Penny was hesitant, afraid that they would mess it up. Patrick, however, encouraged them to give it a try, saying that even if they made mistakes, they would learn something new. Piper and Penny looked at each other, realizing that their brother was right.

Together, they followed Mama Panda's dumpling recipe, carefully mixing the dough and filling and rolling out the wrappers. Patrick watched with interest, offering to help in any way he could. Finally, they steamed the dumplings and placed them on a plate, proud of their culinary creation. As they sat down to eat, Patrick took a bite and exclaimed,

"These are delicious!"

Piper and Penny grinned, happy to have made their brother smile. They knew that taking care of him was their responsibility as siblings, and they were glad to be able to do it well.

From this experience Patrick, Piper and Penny spent time playing board games, reading books, and watching movies. They were careful to make sure Patrick drank plenty of water and took his medicine, checking on him regularly to make sure he was feeling better. When I and my husband returned home, we were impressed to find our cubs were happy. We praised Piper and Penny for their responsible behavior and for taking care of Patrick so well. Piper and Penny smiled, feeling proud of themselves for being good siblings and making their parents proud. They knew that taking care of each other was an important part of being a family, and they were grateful for the opportunity to do it well.

An Argument the Three Siblings Had Over Hide-and-Seek

Patrick, Piper and Penny were playing a game of hide-and-seek in the forest. Patrick was "it" and was trying to find Piper and Penny, who were hiding. As Patrick searched for them, he heard some rustling in the bushes. He thought he had found Piper, so he ran over to the bushes and jumped out to tag her. But when he tagged the figure in the bushes, he realized it was actually Penny. Penny was angry and upset, saying that Patrick had tagged her too hard and hurt her.

Patrick apologized and said that he hadn't meant to hurt Penny. But Penny didn't want to play anymore and stormed off, leaving Patrick and Piper alone in the forest. Piper tried to calm Patrick down, saying that Penny was just upset and would calm down eventually. But Patrick was angry and frustrated, feeling like he couldn't do anything right.

As the afternoon turned into evening, Patrick and Piper grew worried about Penny. They knew they had to find her and make things right. They searched all over the forest, calling Penny's name and looking for any sign of her. Finally, they found her sitting by a stream, looking sad and upset. Patrick approached her and apologized again, saying that he hadn't meant to hurt her. Penny listened, and then apologized for overreacting and storming off.

Patrick and Penny hugged, and Piper joined in. They all felt happy and relieved to be back together, knowing that their sibling bond was stronger than any argument. From then on, they learned the importance of forgiveness and communication. They also learned that it was okay to make mistakes and apologize, as long as they worked to make things right and supported each other.

An Argument the Three Siblings Had with Cleaning up Their Bamboo Forest Home

Another story was about our three children, Patrick, Piper and Penny were tasked with cleaning up their bamboo forest home. Patrick was in charge of sweeping the floors, Piper was in charge of washing the dishes, and Penny was in charge of organizing the books. As they worked, Patrick noticed that Piper had left a pile of dirty dishes in the sink. He asked her to wash them, but Piper said she was busy and that Patrick could wash them himself. Patrick grew frustrated, feeling like he was doing more work than the others. He refused to wash the dishes and instead started sweeping the floor more aggressively, sending dirt and debris flying everywhere.

Piper and Penny tried to reason with Patrick, saying that they all had a part to play in cleaning up the house. But Patrick was too angry to listen and stormed off, leaving Piper and Penny to clean up his mess. The next day, Patrick woke up to find that his broom had been hidden by Piper and Penny. He searched everywhere for it, but couldn't find it. He realized that he had overreacted and acted unfairly towards his siblings.

He went to Piper and Penny and apologized for his behavior, saying that he had let his anger get the best of him. Piper and Penny forgave him, and they all worked together to finish cleaning up the house. They learned to communicate their frustrations and work together to find a solution. They also learned that sometimes it's okay to ask for help and that they were all in this together as a family.

A Story about Honesty

I noticed that her daughter Penny was spending a lot of time with a new friend, a young rabbit named Lulu. The two seemed to get along well and enjoyed spending time together, but I noticed that Lulu had a habit of lying. Penny would come home with stories that didn't quite add up, and when I questioned her about it, Penny would defend Lulu and say that she was just being creative. I knew that I had to teach her daughter about the importance of honesty, but I didn't want to damage her friendship with Lulu.

So I decided to use a story to teach her daughter about honesty. I told Penny the story of a fox who stole food from a farmer's market. The fox was caught by the farmer, but instead of admitting his guilt, the fox blamed it on his friend, a rabbit.

The rabbit was then punished for a crime he didn't commit, and the fox was left feeling guilty for betraying his friend. I used this story to explain that lying not only hurts others, but it can also hurt ourselves.

Penny listened to the story and understood the lesson, but she still didn't want to hurt her friend's feelings by calling her out on her lies. So, I suggested a compromise. I told Penny that she could still be friends with Lulu, but she had to be honest with her and explain how her lies were hurting their friendship. Penny took her mother's advice and talked to Lulu about her lying. To her surprise, Lulu admitted that she had been lying to Penny and apologized for her behavior. The two were able to patch up their friendship and move forward with honesty and trust.

Penny learned about the importance of honesty and how to approach difficult situations with compassion and understanding. And I was proud of our daughter for learning such an important lesson while still maintaining her friendships.

A Story about the Importance of Working Together

Another story was about our three children were playing in the bamboo forest when they came across a group of smaller animals who were trying to build a dam across a nearby stream. The animals were struggling to lift the heavy stones and logs, and the panda siblings could see that they were getting tired. The eldest panda, Patrick, suggested that they help the animals and work together to build the dam. The two younger sisters, however, were hesitant. They wanted to continue playing and didn't see the point in helping the animals.

I noticed the disagreement and approached our children. I explained to them that sometimes, we have to make sacrifices and help others, even if it means putting our own desires aside. To illustrate my point, I told a story about a group of monkeys who were stranded on an island without any food or water. One of the monkeys, a wise old sage, suggested that they all work together to build a boat and sail to the mainland. Some of the monkeys were hesitant and wanted to continue looking for food on the island, but the wise monkey reminded them that they were stronger together and that by working together, they could accomplish great things.

My story resonated with the three siblings, and they decided to help the smaller animals build their dam. They worked together, lifting the heavy stones and logs, and soon the stream was flowing smoothly once again. The smaller animals were grateful for the panda siblings' help, and they thanked them for their kindness. The panda siblings felt a sense of pride and satisfaction knowing that they had made a positive impact in their community. Through this experience, the panda siblings learned about the importance of working together and helping others, even if it means making sacrifices. I was proud of our children for learning such an important lesson and putting it into practice.

A Story about the Importance of Empathy and Compassion

The three panda siblings were out exploring the bamboo forest when they came across a small bird lying on the ground. The bird's wing was broken, and it couldn't fly. The eldest panda, Patrick, suggested that they take the bird to their mother, who was skilled in healing animals. The two younger sisters, however, were hesitant. They didn't want to be late for their playdate with their friends and thought that the bird could fend for itself. I noticed the disagreement and approached our children. I asked them to imagine how they would feel if they were the bird, injured and unable to care for themselves.

Then I reminded our children of the importance of empathy and compassion. I told them a story about a group of animals who were competing in a race. The animals were all trying to reach the finish line first, but one of the animals, a tortoise, was much slower than the others. Many of the animals made fun of the tortoise and didn't think that it had any chance of winning the race. However, one of the animals, a kind-hearted rabbit, saw that the tortoise was struggling and decided to slow down and offer some help. The rabbit ran alongside the tortoise, encouraging it to keep going and offering words of support. In the end, the tortoise and the rabbit crossed the finish line together, both winners in their own right.

My story resonated with the three siblings, and they decided to take the injured bird to me for healing. They worked together to carry the bird back to their home, and their mother was able to mend its wing. The bird flew away, happy and healthy once again. The panda siblings felt a sense of joy and fulfillment knowing that they had helped a creature in need.

Our children learned about the importance of empathy and compassion. They realized that by putting themselves in someone else's shoes, they could better understand their struggles and offer support and kindness.

A Story about Problem Solving

The panda siblings were tasked with building a shelter in the bamboo forest. I had given them a list of materials they needed and explained how to construct a basic shelter. The siblings were excited about the project and got to work immediately. However, they quickly realized that they didn't have enough bamboo to complete the shelter. The eldest sister suggested that they ask their mother for more bamboo, but the boy panda, Patrick insisted that they could find a solution on their own.

The younger sister, Penny had an idea. She remembered seeing some bamboo that had fallen during a storm a few days earlier. She suggested that they go look for it and use it to complete their shelter. Patrick was skeptical, but his sisters convinced him to come along. They searched the forest and eventually found the bamboo they were looking for. They brought it back to their building site and used it to finish their shelter. I was impressed with their resourcefulness and problem-solving skills. I praised them for thinking outside the box and finding a creative solution to their problem. I explained that in life, there are often obstacles and challenges that seem insurmountable, but with perseverance and resourcefulness, we can find a way to overcome them.

The panda siblings learned an important lesson that day. They realized that when faced with a problem, it's important to think creatively and look for solutions that may not be immediately apparent. They also learned that it's okay to ask for help but that finding solutions on their own can be rewarding and empowering. From that day forward, the panda siblings approached problems with a newfound sense of confidence and creativity. They knew that they could rely on their own problem-solving skills to overcome any obstacle that came their way.

Another Story about Problem Solving

That afternoon, the panda siblings were playing in the bamboo forest when they stumbled upon a lost baby bird. It had fallen out of its nest and was chirping frantically, trying to find its way back home. The siblings knew that the baby bird needed their help. They looked around for the bird's nest but couldn't find it. They asked some of the other animals in the forest if they knew where it was, but nobody had seen it. The siblings knew that they needed to act fast to help the baby bird. The eldest sister, Piper, suggested that they build a nest for the baby bird. The boy panda, Patrick thought that was a good idea, but the younger sister pointed out that they didn't know how to build a bird's nest. They needed to find a way to learn how to do it.

The siblings put their heads together and came up with a plan. They remembered that there was an old bird's nest in a nearby tree that had been abandoned by its inhabitants. They decided to study the nest and try to figure out how to build one like it. They spent the next few hours carefully examining the abandoned nest. They took note of the materials used, the shape of the nest, and how it was attached to the tree. They also observed other birds in the forest and took note of their nests. With this information, the siblings went to work building a nest for the baby bird. They used twigs, leaves, and grass to construct a cozy little nest, and they attached it to a nearby tree branch. The baby bird was hesitant at first, but eventually, it hopped into the nest and snuggled down.

The siblings were proud of their work and relieved that they could help the baby bird. I was also proud of them and praised them for their resourcefulness and problem-solving skills. The panda siblings learned that when faced with a complex problem, it's important to break it down into smaller parts and approach it methodically. They also learned that sometimes, the solution may not be immediately apparent, and it's important to think creatively and outside the box to find a solution.

A Story about Diligence

Our family was out foraging for bamboo shoots when we noticed a group of squirrel's frantically collecting nuts for the winter. My husband pointed out the squirrels' diligence to his children and explained how their hard work and planning would help them survive the winter. He then asked his children how they could apply the same principles to our own lives. The eldest daughter suggested that they could start preparing for the next season by collecting and storing bamboo shoots, just like the squirrels were doing with their nuts.

My husband was pleased with her suggestion and encouraged his other two children to think about how they could also be diligent in their daily lives. The boy panda suggested that he could start practicing his martial arts every day to improve his skills, while the youngest daughter suggested that she could study her schoolwork more diligently to get better grades. My husband praised their ideas and reminded them that diligence was not just about working hard, but also about working smart. He encouraged them to be organized and focused in their tasks and to prioritize the most important things in their lives.

Over the next few weeks, the siblings put their ideas into action. The eldest daughter collected and stored bamboo shoots for the winter, while the boy panda practiced his martial arts every day. The youngest daughter studied diligently and saw an improvement in her grades. My husband was proud of his children's diligence and reminded them that hard work and planning were essential for success in life. He also reminded them that it was important to take breaks and rest when needed, as overworking could lead to burnout and exhaustion. Our children learned that diligence was not just about working hard, but also about planning, organization, and focus. They learned that by being diligent, they could achieve their goals and make a positive impact on their lives and the lives of those around them.

Another Story About Diligent

Our panda family decided to take a trip to the nearby river for a picnic. My husband was responsible for preparing the food and packing the picnic basket, while I was in charge of organizing the transportation and making sure everyone had their necessary supplies. As we were getting ready to leave, my husband realized that he had forgotten to bring drinks for everyone. He quickly ran to the kitchen to grab some drinks but found that they were out of their favorite juice.

Instead of giving up and telling everyone that they had to go without drinks, my husband decided to be diligent and find a solution. He quickly thought of an alternative plan and decided to make some fresh juice from the fruits that they had in the kitchen. My husband spent the next hour carefully cutting and juicing the fruits, making sure that the juice was the perfect consistency and taste. When he was done, he proudly presented the freshly made juice to his family.

I was impressed by the father's diligence and praised him for finding a creative solution to the problem. I reminded our children that being diligent meant not giving up when faced with challenges and finding ways to overcome them. Our children learned that being diligent was not just about working hard, but also about being resourceful and finding solutions to problems. They learned that by being diligent, they could turn challenges into opportunities and make the most out of any situation. Our children were more aware of their own diligence and started applying it in their daily lives. They realized that with diligence and perseverance, they could achieve great things and overcome any obstacle that came their way.

One More About Diligent

My husband was working in the garden when he noticed that the bamboo shoots in the garden had started to wither and die. He quickly realized that there was a problem with the soil and that we needed to take immediate action to save our garden. He called his children and explained the situation to them. He told them that they needed to find a way to improve the soil in the garden, but they didn't have any extra money to buy new soil.

The three siblings put their heads together and started brainstorming ideas. The eldest suggested that they start composting to create their own fertilizer, while the middle child suggested planting cover crops to help improve the soil. The youngest suggested that they try to find some natural sources of fertilizer around their house, like coffee grounds and eggshells.

My husband was impressed by his children's ingenuity and encouraged them to try all of their ideas. They worked hard for several days, composting and planting cover crops and using natural fertilizers to improve the soil in their garden.

After several weeks of hard work, we were able to restore our garden to its former glory. The bamboo shoots were growing strong and healthy, and our family was able to enjoy fresh bamboo shoots from our own garden. My husband was proud of his children's problem-solving skills and their dedication to finding a solution to the problem. He reminded them that sometimes, the most challenging problems can be solved with a little creativity and ingenuity. Our children learned an important lesson about perseverance and creativity, and how they could apply these qualities to any challenge that they may face in life. They realized that with determination and hard work, they could overcome any obstacle and achieve their goals.

About Leadership Story, How My Husband Teach Our Children

My husband knew that leadership skills were important for his children's future success, so he decided to teach them about leadership in a practical way. He took his children on a hike through the bamboo forest. As they were walking, they came across a group of animals who were lost and looking for their way back to their homes. My husband saw this as an opportunity to teach his children about leadership.

He asked his children to take charge of the situation and help the lost animals find their way back home. At first, the children were hesitant and unsure of what to do, but their father encouraged them to take the lead. Patrick, the eldest child took charge and started asking the lost animals about their homes and where they had come from. Piper, the middle child helped by making a map of the area and plotting out the animals' locations. The youngest child, Penny helped by collecting bamboo shoots to give the animals as food for their journey home.

With the children's leadership and teamwork, they were able to guide the lost animals back to their homes safely. My husband was proud of his children's leadership skills and praised them for their hard work and dedication.

He explained to them that leadership is not just about being in charge, but also about being responsible and caring for those around you. He reminded them that as they grow up and take on more responsibilities, they will need to use their leadership skills to make a positive impact on the world around them. The panda siblings learned an important lesson about leadership that day. They realized that leadership is not just a title, but a responsibility to guide and help those around them. They were inspired to continue developing their leadership skills and use them to make a positive impact.

Another Leadership Story, How My Husband Teach Our Children

My husband wanted to challenge his children's leadership skills even further, so he organized a camping trip for the family in the forest. During the camping trip, the father panda pretended to become ill and needed to be taken to the nearest medical center. He told his children that they would need to work together to get him to the medical center safely. The eldest child, Patrick took charge of the situation and delegated tasks to his younger siblings. Piper took responsibility for gathering supplies and packing them in the backpack. Penny, the youngest child helped by keeping her father's spirits up and providing encouragement.

The journey to the medical center was not an easy one. The forest was dense and the path was treacherous. Along the way, they encountered obstacles such as fallen trees and steep hills. The children had to work together to find solutions to these challenges and keep their father safe. Despite the challenges, the children showed great leadership skills and were able to get their father to the medical center safely. The doctors were impressed with their teamwork and leadership skills, and praised them for their bravery and determination.

My husband was proud of his children's leadership skills and praised them for their hard work and dedication. He explained to them that leadership is not just about delegating tasks, but also about being able to adapt to new situations and find solutions to challenges. The panda siblings learned an important lesson about leadership and problem-solving that day. They realized that in order to be effective leaders, they needed to be able to work together as a team, adapt to new situations, and find solutions to challenges. They were inspired to continue developing their leadership and problem-solving skills, and to use them to make a positive impact on their community.

<u>One More Leadership Story, How My Husband Teach Our Children</u>

My husband, the father panda wanted to teach his children about the importance of leading by example. He knew that children learn by observing their parents' behavior, so he decided to show his children the value of hard work and dedication.

My husband took his children to the local bamboo grove. He explained to them that bamboo was an important resource for their family and for the entire forest ecosystem. He showed them how to identify the best bamboo shoots and how to cut them down without damaging the grove. My husband then picked up his own bamboo cutting tool and began to work alongside his children. He showed them how to work efficiently and with care, always paying attention to the health of the grove and the quality of the bamboo shoots.

As they worked, the father panda shared stories of his own childhood and the lessons he had learned about hard work and dedication. He explained that the most successful leaders were those who led by example and demonstrated a strong work ethic and commitment to their goals. The children were inspired by their father's example and began to work even harder, eager to show their own dedication and commitment. They worked side by side with their father, cutting down the bamboo shoots and carrying them back to their home.

At the end of the day, my husband praised his children for their hard work and dedication. He reminded them that leadership is not just about giving orders, but also about setting a positive example and inspiring others to work hard and strive for excellence. The panda siblings learned an important lesson that day about the value of hard work and dedication. They realized that in order to be successful leaders, they needed to demonstrate a strong work ethic and a commitment to their goals. They were inspired by their father's example and committed to leading by example themselves, both in their family and in their community.

Story about Looking After Each Other Between Siblings

Our panda family was gathered in the living room, and the parents noticed that their children were playing separately. The eldest, Patrick, was playing with his toys in one corner, while his sisters, Piper and Penny, were playing with their dolls in another corner. The parents were worried that their children were not spending enough time together and not learning the importance of looking after each other.

So, we decided to come up with a fun activity that would teach their children about the importance of helping and looking after each other. We gathered our children together and told them that they were going to have a scavenger hunt. But, there was a catch - they had to work together to find all the items on the list.

The list included things like a red leaf, a feather, a pinecone, and a smooth rock. The children were excited to begin the scavenger hunt, but the parents reminded them that they had to work together to find all the items on the list. The children work as one team of three, Patrick, Piper and Penny.

As they began the scavenger hunt, the children soon realized that they needed each other's help to find all the items on the list. For example, Patrick was taller and could reach the higher branches of the trees, so he helped his sister to find the red leaf. Piper was able to spot a feather on the ground, and she helped her sister to identify it on the list. They also encouraged each other and offered words of support when they found an item, saying things like

"Great job! We're getting closer to finding everything on the list."

After some time, the children were able to find all the items on the list, and they returned to their parents with big smiles on their faces. We praised our children for working together and told them that they had successfully completed the scavenger hunt. We then explained to our children that they needed to look after each other just like they did during the scavenger hunt. We reminded our children that they were a family, and it was important to help and support each other, no matter what.

Our children started to spend more time together and looked after each other more. They began to understand the importance of working as a team and how helping each other can make things easier and more fun. My husband and I, as their parents were happy to see our children learning and growing together, and they knew that their lesson on looking after each other had been successful.

Another Story about Looking After Each Other Between Siblings to Work Together As a Team

One memorable day, the three Panda siblings were playing in the forest when they came across a steep hill. They decided to climb it together, but as they reached the top, they began to argue about which way to go next. Patrick, the eldest brother, who was always confident and outspoken, suggested they go left. But the middle sister, Piper, disagreed, insisting they should go right instead. The youngest sister, Penny, who was often caught in the middle of their arguments, didn't know which way to choose.

As they continued to argue, they failed to notice that the sky had grown dark and storm clouds were gathering overhead. Suddenly, a bolt of lightning struck a nearby tree, causing it to fall and block their path back down the hill. Realizing they were stuck at the top of the hill, the siblings knew they needed to work together to find a way back down. However, they were still so caught up in their argument that they couldn't agree on anything.

My husband and I soon heard the commotion and came to see what was going on. Seeing that our children were in trouble, we sat down with them and began to teach them about the importance of teamwork. My husband and I explained that sometimes, disagreements are inevitable, but it's important to listen to each other's ideas and come up with a solution together. We encouraged our children to work as a team and use their individual strengths to help each other.

Taking their parents' advice to heart, the siblings finally started to work together. The eldest brother, Patrick used his strength to move the fallen tree out of the way, while the middle sister used her quick thinking to create a makeshift path down the hill. The youngest sister, Penny, who was often overlooked, used her keen observation skills to spot any potential dangers along the way. Together, they successfully made their way down the hill and back home. After that day, the siblings learned the importance of working together as a team and helping each other, even when they didn't see eye to eye. They became closer as siblings and made a promise to always listen to each other's ideas and work together as a team.

<u>One More Story about Looking After Each Other Between Siblings to Work Together As a Team</u>

Our Panda family was planning a picnic. The parents had to attend an important meeting, so they asked their children to pack the picnic basket and meet them at the park. The Panda siblings were excited about the picnic, but they had different ideas about what to bring. The eldest brother, Patrick, being the most responsible, wanted to pack healthy food, like fruits and vegetables. The youngest sister, on the other hand, wanted to bring her favorite snacks, like chips and candy. And the middle sister, Piper, wanted to bring a mix of both.

They started arguing about what to pack, each insisting on their own choices. They couldn't agree and ended up packing their own separate bags. When they arrived at the park, they realized they forgot some important items, like the plates and utensils. They also didn't have enough food for everyone, and the bags were disorganized.

At first, they were disappointed and started blaming each other for the mistakes. But then, they remembered what their parents had taught them about working together and problem-solving.

The eldest brother suggested they combine the food from all three bags, and they could share and enjoy each other's favorite snacks. The middle sister came up with the idea of using leaves as makeshift plates, and they used sticks as utensils. The youngest sister offered to organize the bags and make sure they had everything they needed. They worked together as a team, and soon, the picnic was set up and ready to enjoy. They realized that by working together, they were able to create a much better picnic experience than they would have alone. They even discovered that they liked some of each other's favorite foods and learned to appreciate each other's differences.

When my husband and I arrived, we were impressed with how well our children had worked together and solved their problems. We praised them for their teamwork and reminded them that they could achieve anything if they worked together. Patrick, Piper and our youngest child, Penny learned to appreciate each other's strengths and work together as a team, not just for picnics, but in all aspects of their lives.

A Story About Not Easy To Give Up Even Though the Condition Was Too Difficult

Our Panda family decided to go on a picnic. We packed a delicious lunch, and set out for a nearby forest. The weather was warm, and we were looking forward to a fun day in the outdoors. As we were walking along a trail, we suddenly heard a loud noise. It sounded like a large tree had fallen somewhere nearby. We stopped in our tracks, and looked around for the source of the sound. After a few moments, we spotted a clearing up ahead. As we approached, we saw that a huge tree had indeed fallen across the trail, blocking our way forward. The tree was so large that we couldn't climb over it, and the trunk was too thick to move.

Our children were disappointed that their picnic plans had been ruined. They started to grumble and complain, saying that it was too difficult to find another place for a picnic. My husband and I encouraged them to think of a solution. We reminded them that it was important to never give up, even in difficult situations. Patrick, Piper and Penny were unsure, but my husband and I insisted that they keep looking for a place to have their picnic.

Our family continued to walk along the trail, looking for a new spot to have our picnic. We came across a small stream, and a grassy area next to it. We suggested that they could have their picnic there. The children were hesitant at first, saying that it wasn't the same as their original plan. But we encouraged them to be flexible, and to appreciate the beauty of their new surroundings.

While we ate our lunch, our family started to enjoy themselves. Our children listened to the sounds of the forest, and watched as birds flew overhead. They realized that their new spot was just as beautiful as the original plan, and that they had made the best of a difficult situation.

The children learned an important lesson that day. They learned that it's important to never give up, even when things don't go as planned. They learned to be flexible, and to appreciate the beauty in unexpected places. Our children learned, whenever they faced a difficult situation, they remembered the lesson they learned on their picnic. They faced each challenge with determination and a positive attitude, and they never gave up.

<u>Another Story about Not Easy To Give Up Even Though the Condition Was Too Difficult</u>

It was a beautiful summer day in the bamboo forest, and our Panda family was enjoying a picnic near a river. We were all having a great time until they noticed that the water level in the river was rising rapidly. We quickly packed up our things and headed back to our home.

As we arrived at our home, Patrick, Piper and Penny at the same time realized that the rising water level was causing a lot of damage. The water had flooded their garden and was getting dangerously close to their home. Our family knew that we had to take action quickly to prevent any further damage.

The eldest children, panda boy, Patrick, suggested building a dam to divert the water away from their home. The two younger pandas were hesitant, but their parents encouraged them to give it a try.

For the next week, the family worked tirelessly to build a dam. They worked together, digging and piling up dirt and rocks to create the barrier. It was hard work, and they had to work long hours every day to get it done. They faced several challenges along the way, including a heavy rainstorm that nearly washed away their progress.

Despite the setbacks, our family refused to give up. We continued to work hard, encouraging each other and staying positive even when things seemed hopeless.

Finally, after a week of hard work, the dam was complete. The water was successfully diverted away from our home, and the damage was minimal. Our Panda family was exhausted but overjoyed at our success. We celebrated by having a big feast together, enjoying the fruits of their labor.

My husband and I used this as an opportunity to teach our children the importance of never giving up, even when things seem impossible. We also reminded Patrick, Piper and Penny that by working together as a team, they can overcome any obstacle. From that day forward, our Panda family was even closer than before. They had learned to rely on each other, to support each other, and to never give up, no matter how difficult the challenge may be.

One More Story About Not Easy To Give Up Even Though the Condition Was Too Difficult

This story is a bit more complex story, one day, a major storm hit the forest where our panda family lived. It was a particularly strong storm, and it caused a lot of damage to the trees and the homes of the forest animals. Our Panda family's home was also affected, and the roof of our home was severely damaged.

My husband and I also our three siblings tried our best to fix the roof, but we realized that it was beyond our abilities. We needed to call in a professional to fix the roof, but with the storm still raging on, it was impossible to get anyone to come and help. Our family was left with a difficult decision:

"Wait out the storm and risk more damage to our home, or try to fix the roof ourselves"

My husband knew that the second option was risky, but he also knew that we couldn't afford to wait any longer. So, my husband called a family meeting and explained the situation to his children. He told them that they were going to work together to fix the roof, and that it was going to be a difficult and dangerous task. The children were hesitant at first, but they trusted their father and knew that they needed to do something to protect their home.

My husband divided the tasks among his children. The eldest, the Panda boy, Patrick, was responsible for climbing up to the roof and securing the ladder. The two younger sisters were responsible for passing tools and materials up to their brother. The father and mother were responsible for guiding and supervising the process.

It was a challenging task, and the storm didn't make it any easier. The wind was strong, and the rain was heavy, making it difficult for the children to pass the materials up to their brother on the roof. However, they didn't give up. They communicated and worked together, using their creativity and problem-solving skills to come up with solutions to the obstacles they faced.

It took them a week to fix the roof, but they finally succeeded. They were tired and exhausted, but they were also proud of what they had accomplished as a family. They had worked together to overcome a difficult challenge, and they had succeeded. From this experience, our family knew that we could overcome any challenge as long as we worked together. Our children had learned the value of teamwork and perseverance, and they knew that these qualities would help them in any situation they might face in the future.

CHAPTER XII
ANOTHER FACTS OF PANDA

There are several facts of Panda:

1. Pandas are one of the world's most beloved animals. They are known for their distinctive black and white fur, and are often depicted as gentle, playful creatures. People all over the world love pandas, and they are often seen as symbols of peace and harmony. In China, pandas are considered a national treasure, and are protected by law.

2. Pandas are native to China, where they are found in the mountainous regions of Sichuan, Shaanxi, and Gansu provinces. These areas are known for their bamboo forests, which provide the pandas with the food they need to survive. Pandas have lived in China for millions of years, and are an important part of the country's cultural heritage.

3. Pandas are classified as a type of bear, although they have some unique characteristics that set them apart from other bears. For example, pandas have a special adaptation in their digestive system that allows them to break down the tough fibers in bamboo. They also have a "false thumb," which is actually an extension of their wrist bone that they use to grasp bamboo stalks.

4. One of the most distinctive features of pandas is their diet. They

are almost entirely herbivorous, and their diet consists mainly of bamboo. They eat up to 40 pounds of bamboo every day, which is a lot for an animal their size. To help them digest the tough bamboo fibers, pandas have a special digestive system that breaks down the bamboo in their stomachs.

5. Pandas are also known for their adorable appearance. They have large, round heads, and their black and white fur is soft and fluffy. They have a distinctive "panda" face, with black patches around their eyes and ears. The black and white coloring of their fur is thought to help them blend in with their surroundings in the forest.

6. Baby pandas, or cubs, are particularly cute. They are born tiny and helpless, weighing only a few ounces. They are completely dependent on their mothers for the first few months of their lives. During this time, the mother panda provides her cub with milk and keeps it warm and safe. Baby pandas stay with their mothers for up to two years before they become independent.

7. Pandas are social animals, and live in groups in the wild. These groups, known as "communities," can consist of up to 15 pandas. Within these communities, pandas communicate with each other through a variety of vocalizations, including bleats, moans, and chirps. They also use body language, such as tail wags and head nods, to communicate.

8. Pandas are also excellent climbers. They have strong limbs and sharp claws, which they use to climb trees and bamboo stalks. They are particularly skilled at climbing when they are young. In fact, baby pandas are often seen climbing on their mothers' backs as they move through the forest.

9. Despite their cute appearance, pandas are actually quite strong. Adult pandas can weigh up to 300 pounds, and can run at speeds of up to 20 miles per hour.

Don't miss out!

Visit the website below and you can sign up to receive emails whenever The Blessed Creation publishes a new book. There's no charge and no obligation.

https://books2read.com/r/B-A-XGAX-JVJGC

BOOKS 2 READ

Connecting independent readers to independent writers.

About the Author

ABOUT THE AUTHOR

The Blessed Creation is The Home of one Family with several persons. All Family Members grew a passion to empower people to live life to the fullest. We believe that everyone has the opportunity to get the right support around them.

The Blessed Creation believe that we will empower people for BETTER LIFE by sharing stories through publishing the great and awesome books. It is a GIFT to the WORLD.

Everyone has biggest passion about writing and creation for everything which are very good to share to the World. One of us is a freelance editor, has a Graduate Certificate of Editing and Publishing. This person has biggest passion to get perfecting book manuscripts for publication. He is passionate about art, including how to make beautiful book to share.

We have several artist who thinking outside the square and giving us a lot of ideas for our potential Buyers to enjoy.

Want to contact us ? Just drop an email to: theblessedcreation17@gmail.com